Flower Arrangements

A hand-drawn coloring book

Queenie Wong

ISBN-13: 978-1535334853
ISBN-10: 1535334851
First published in United States in 2016
Illustrations by Queenie Wong
Wonger0050@yahoo.com.hk

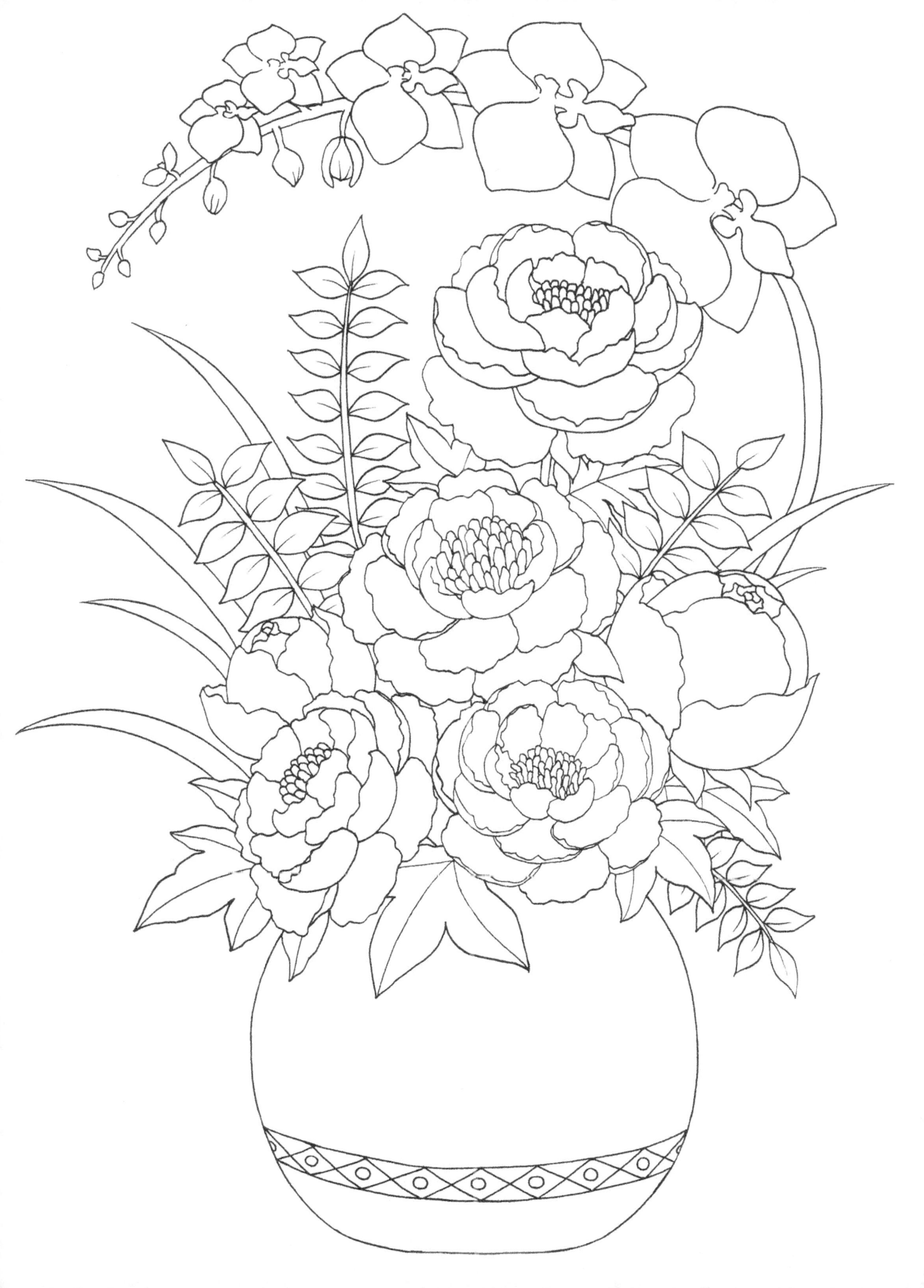

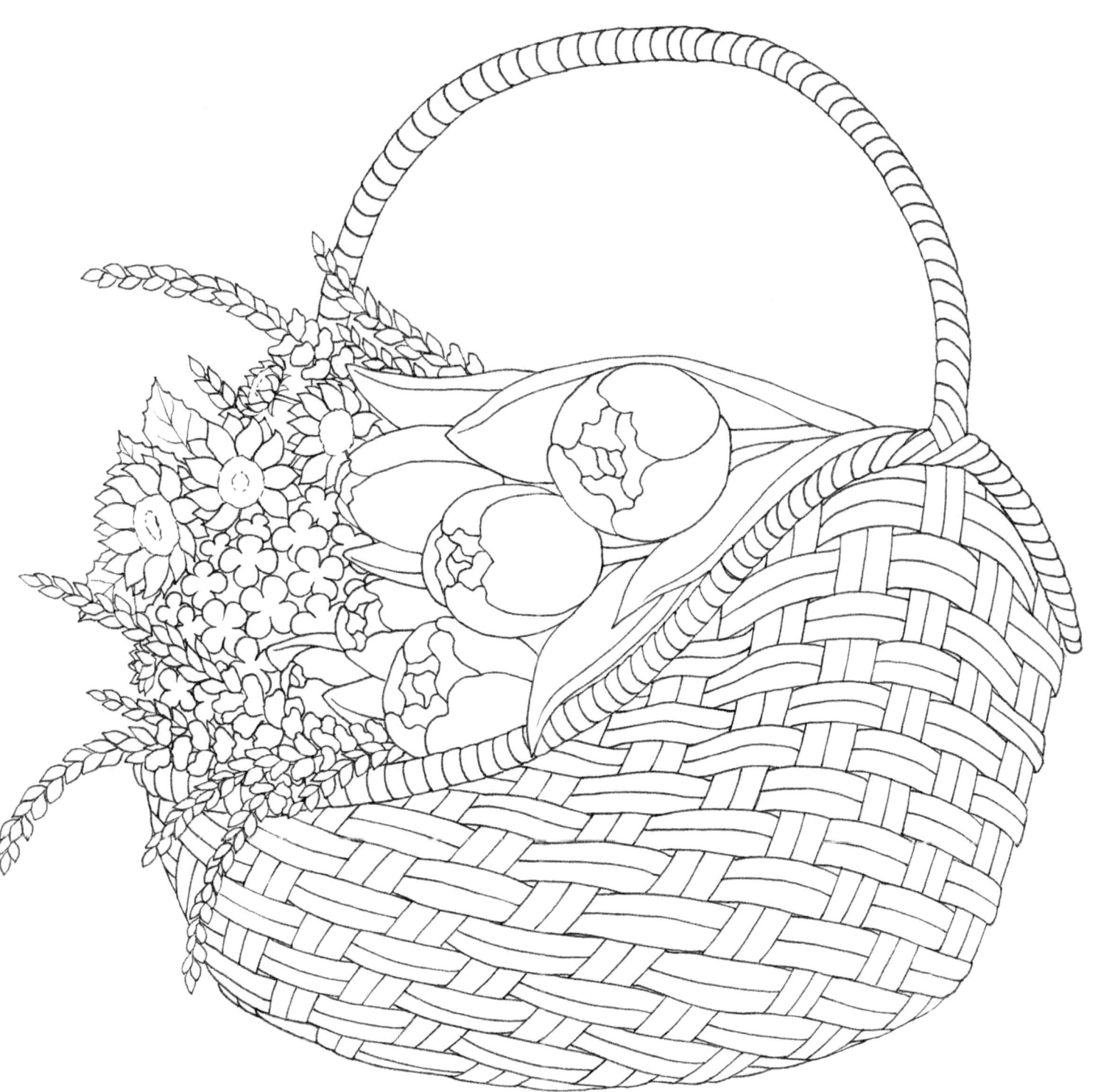

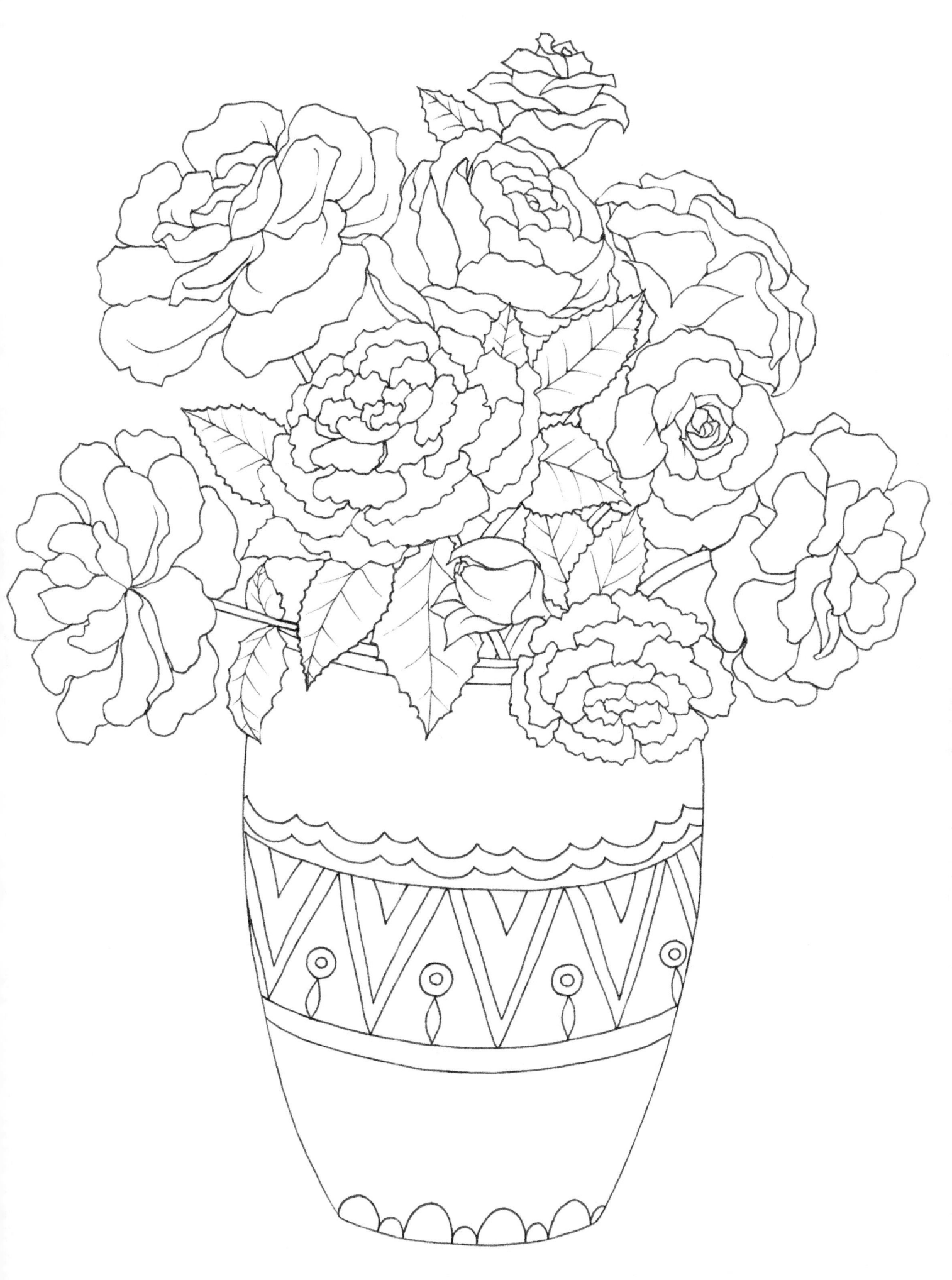

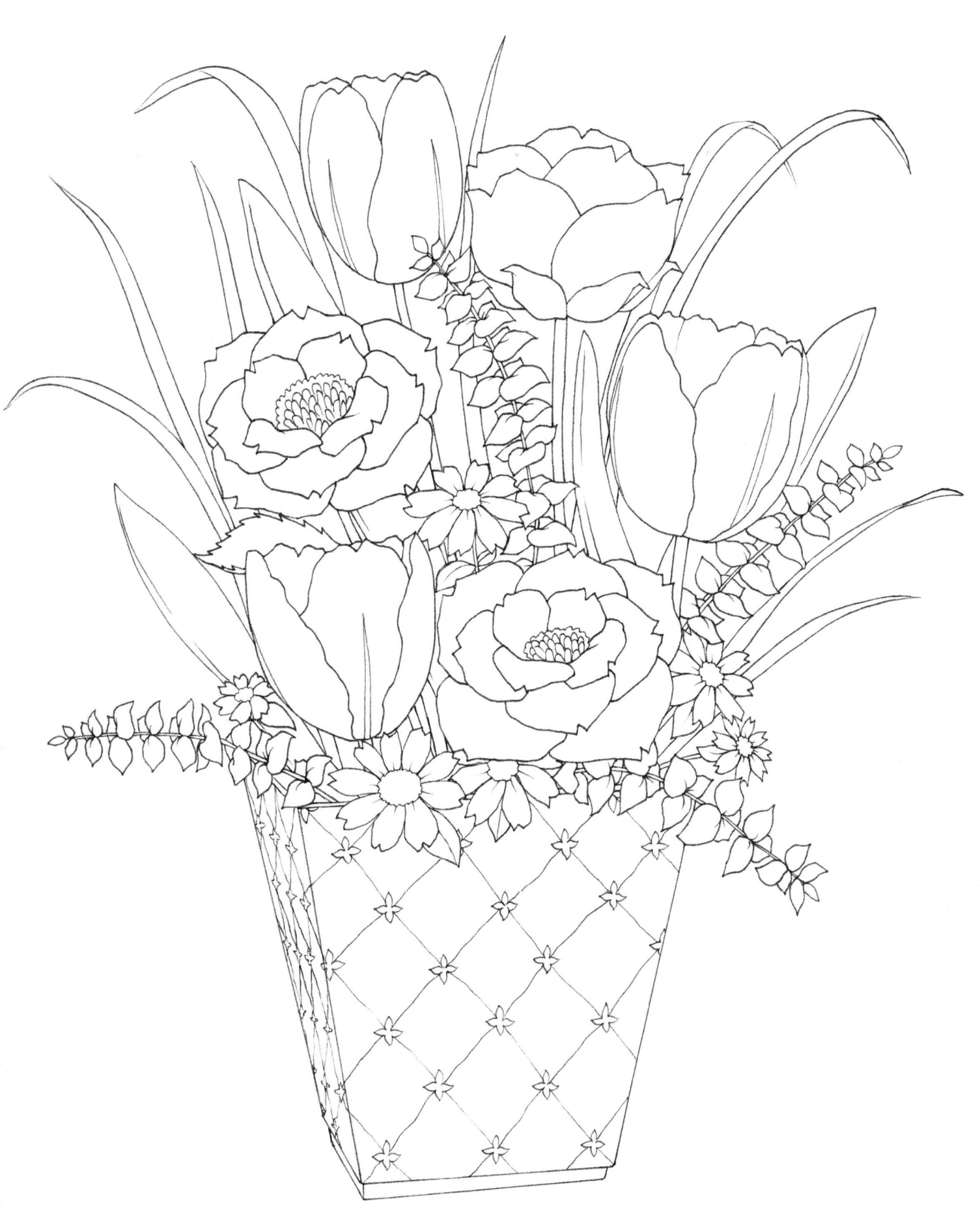

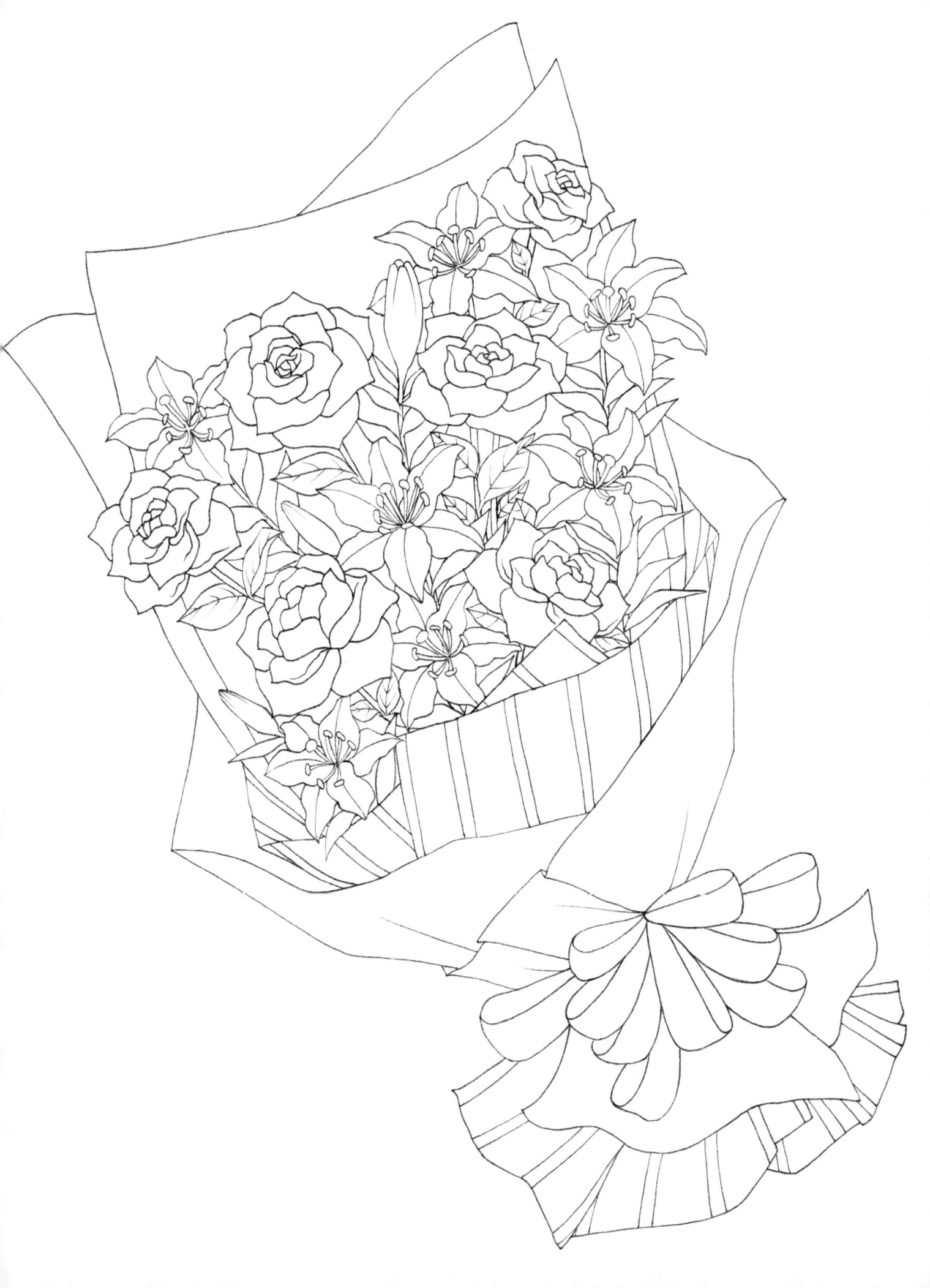

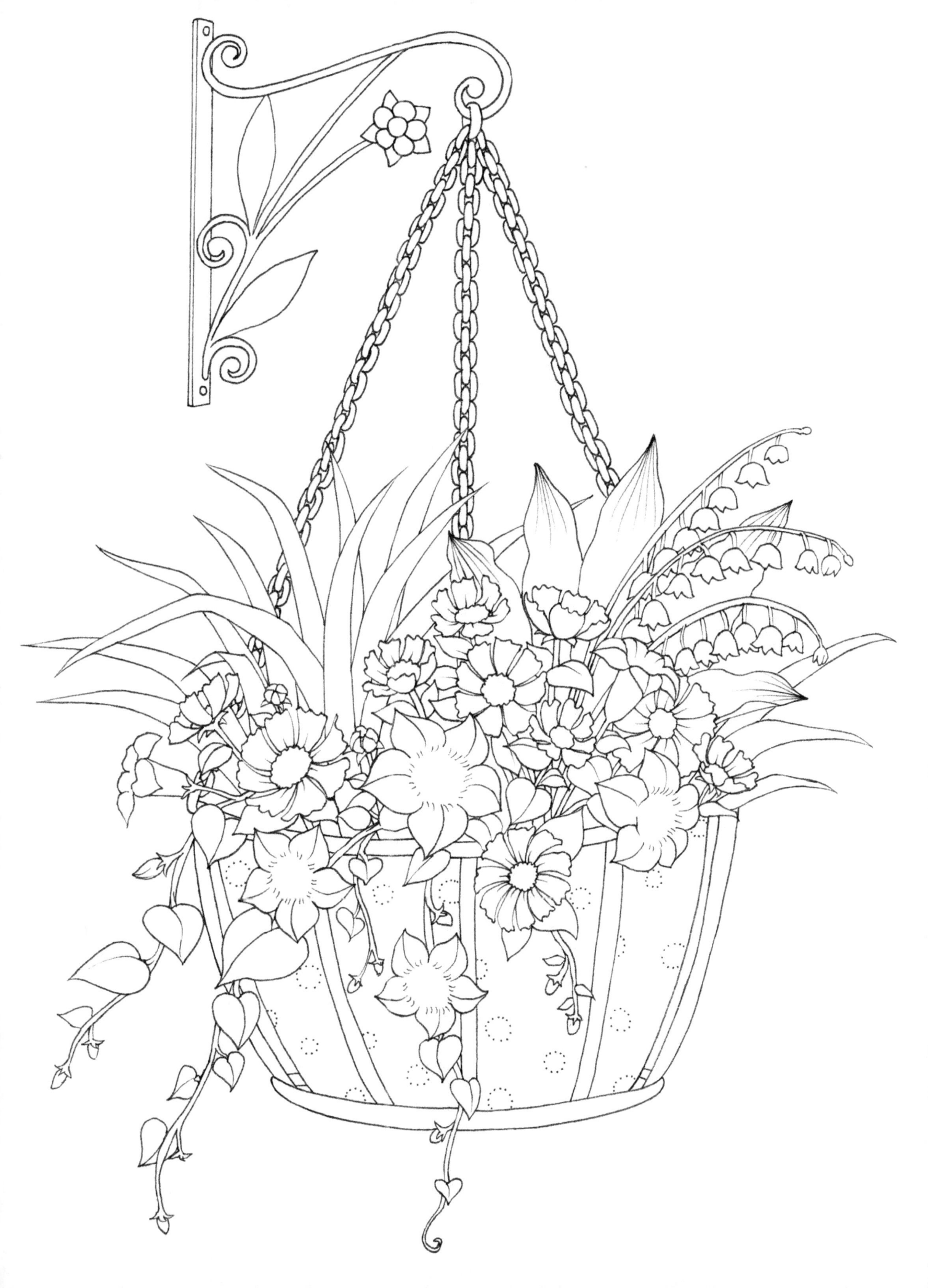

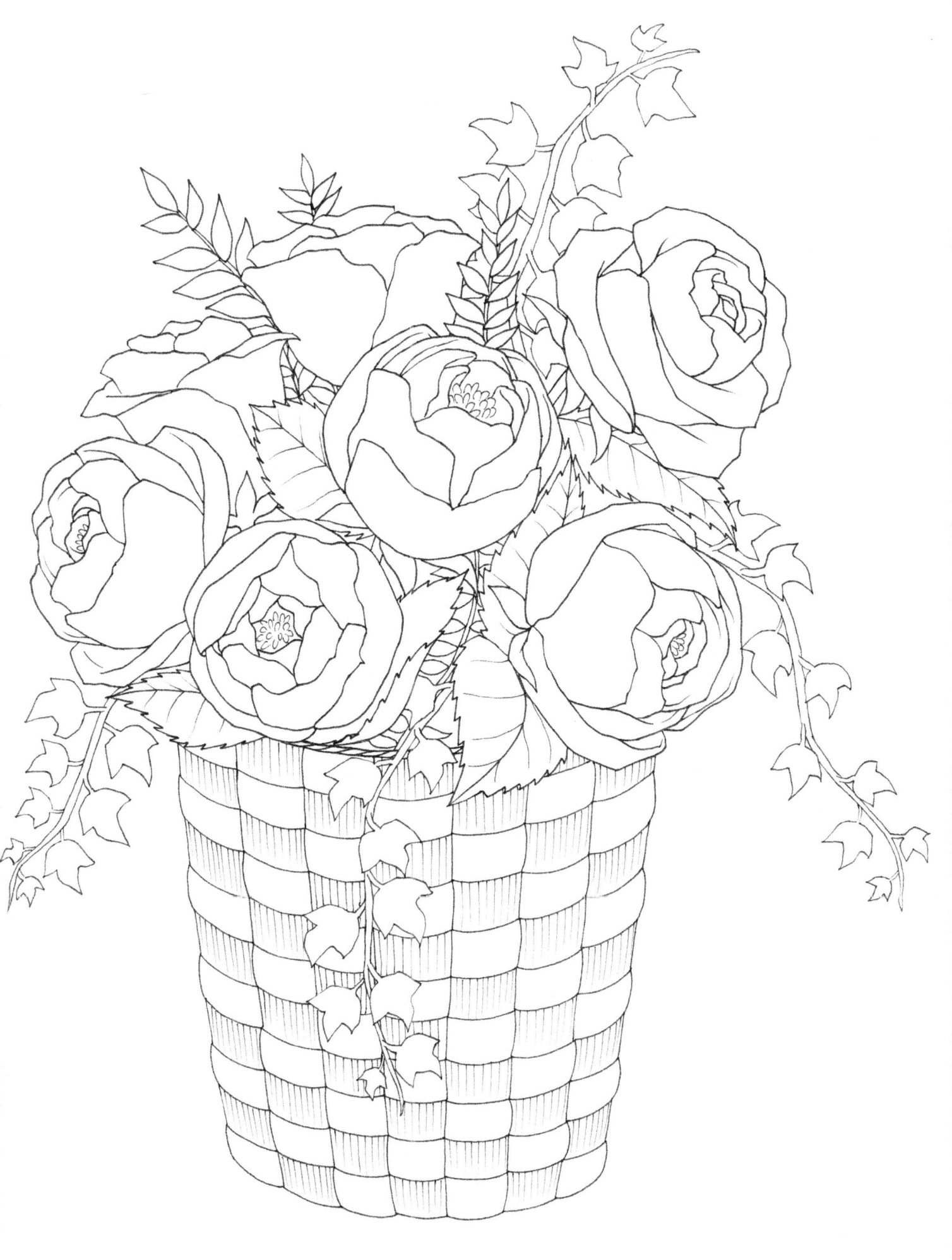

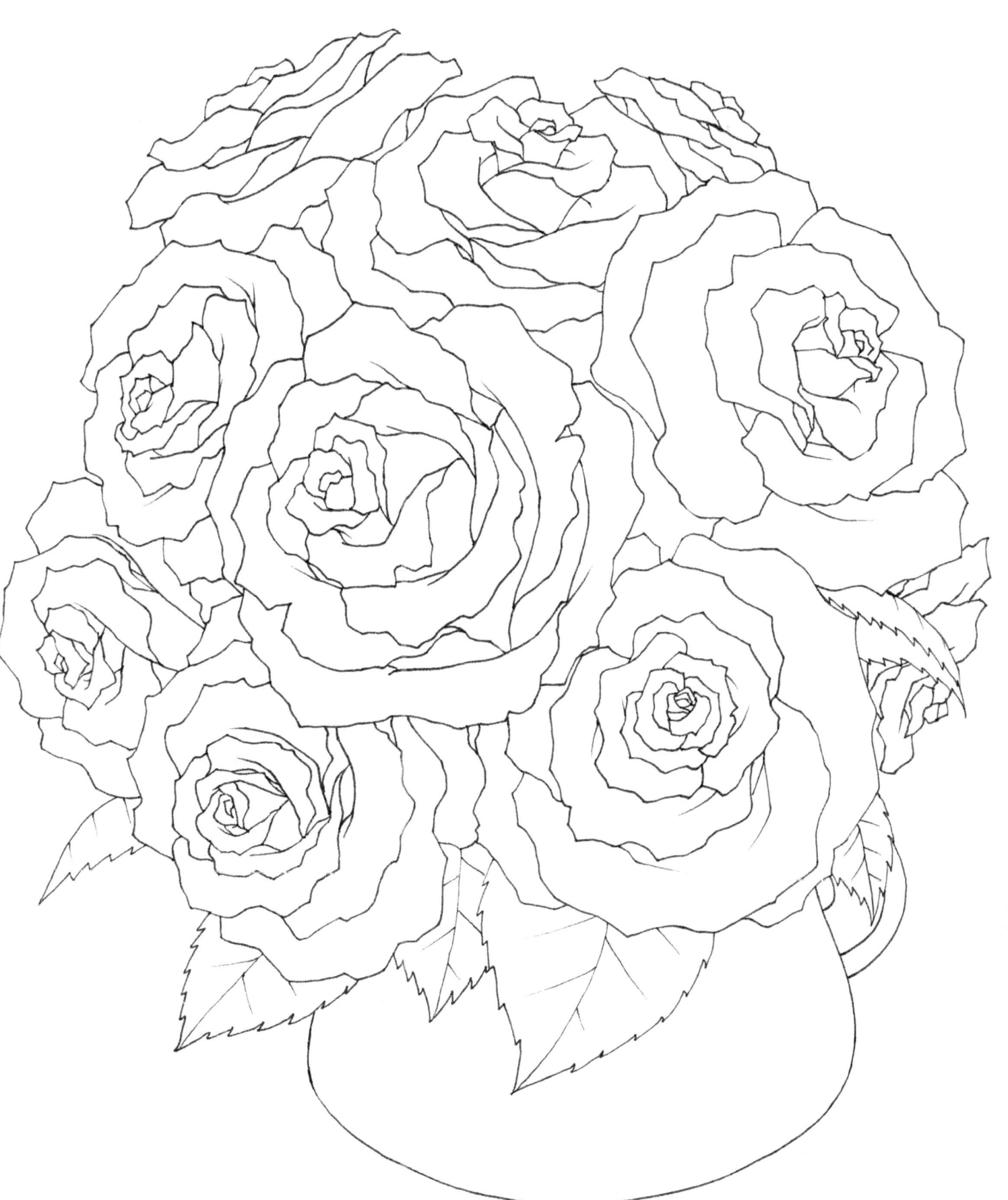

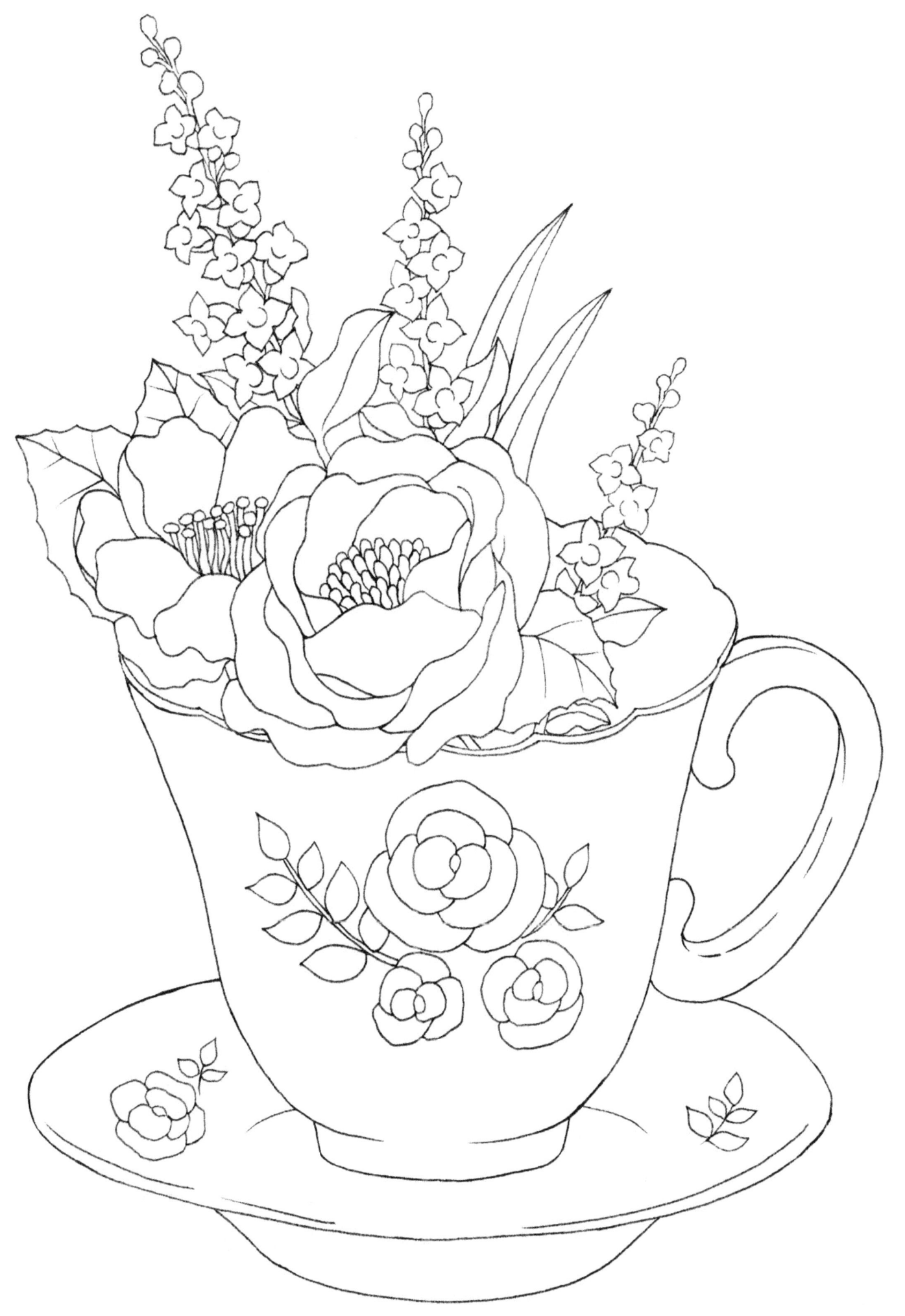

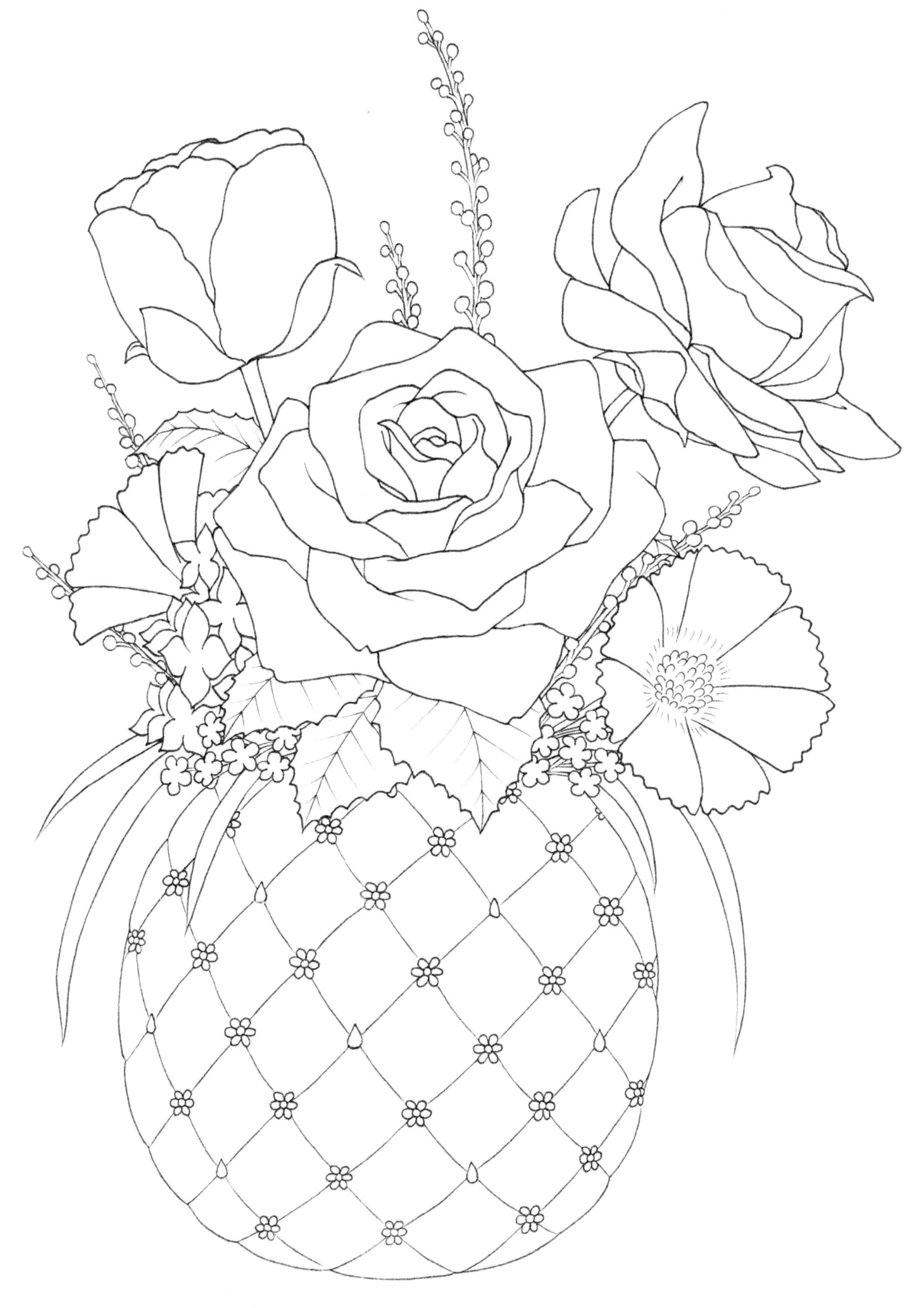

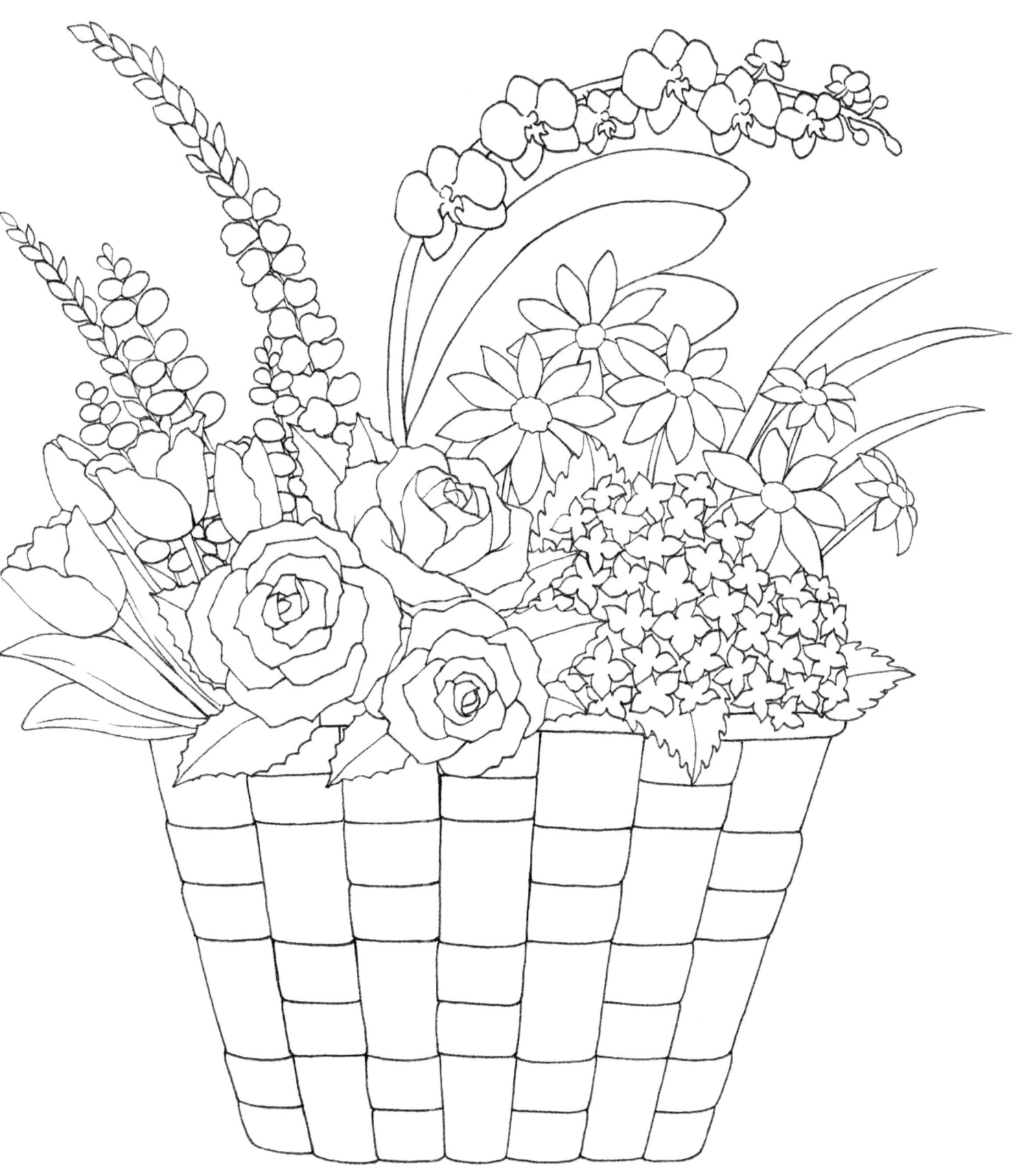

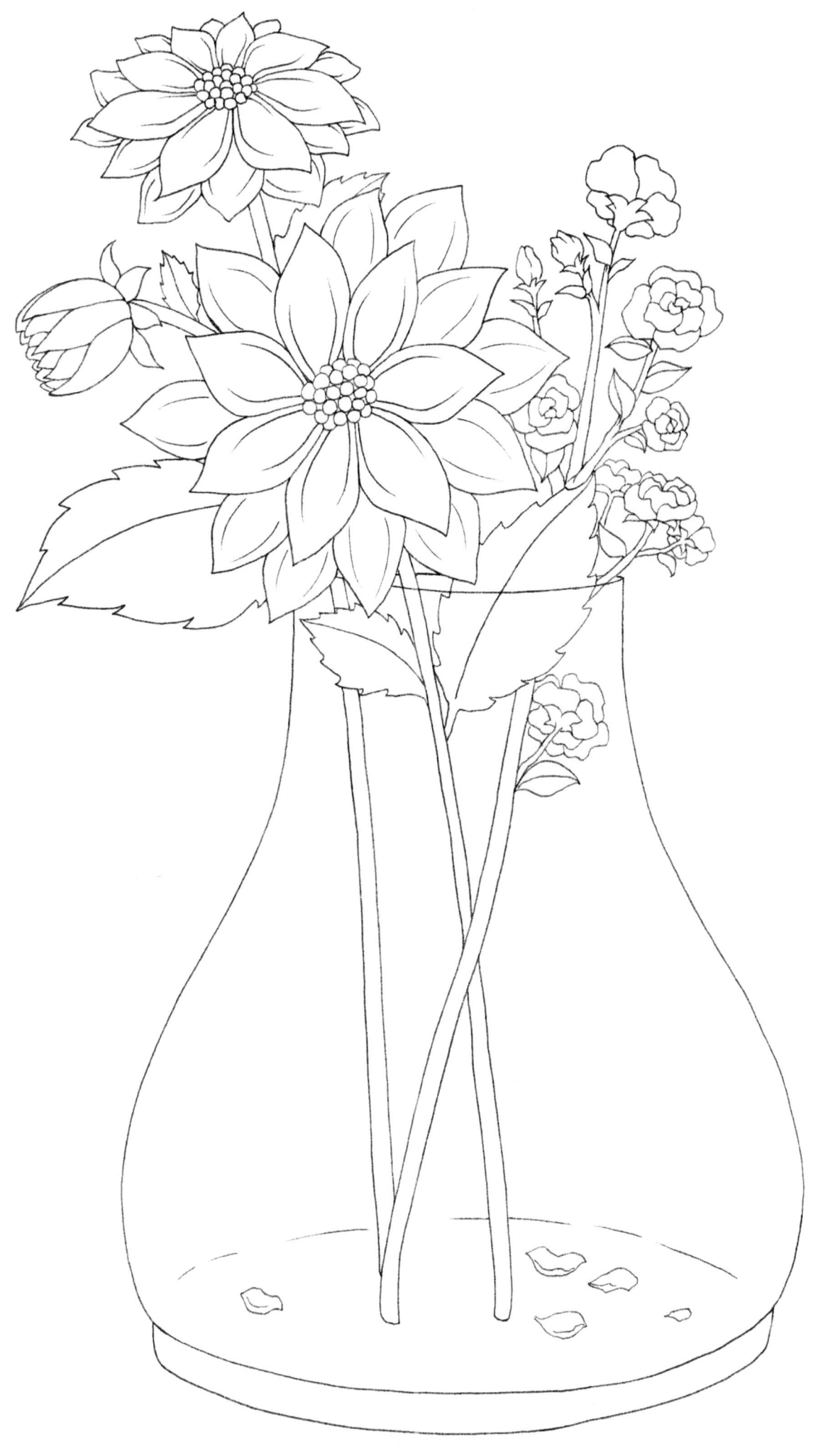

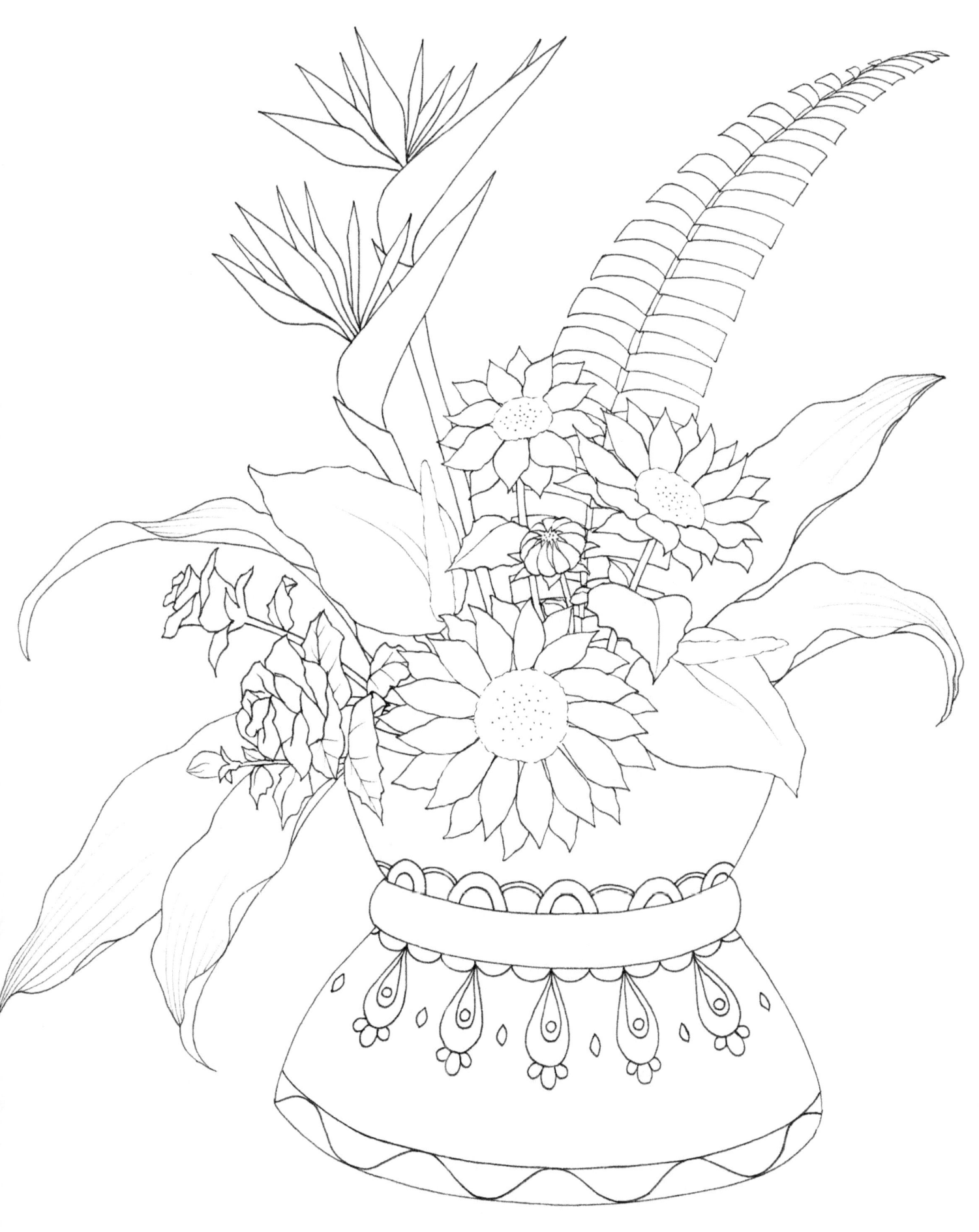

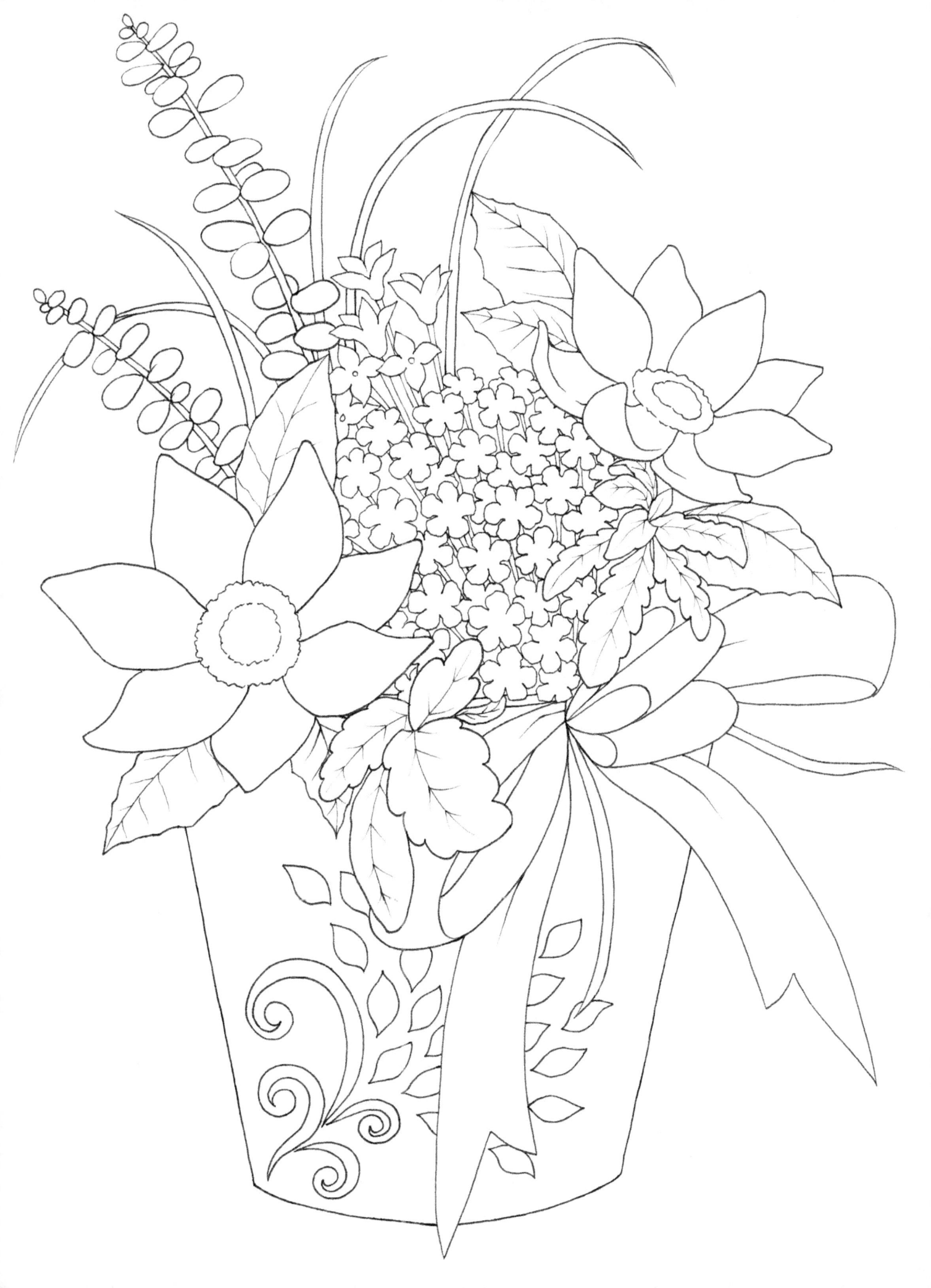

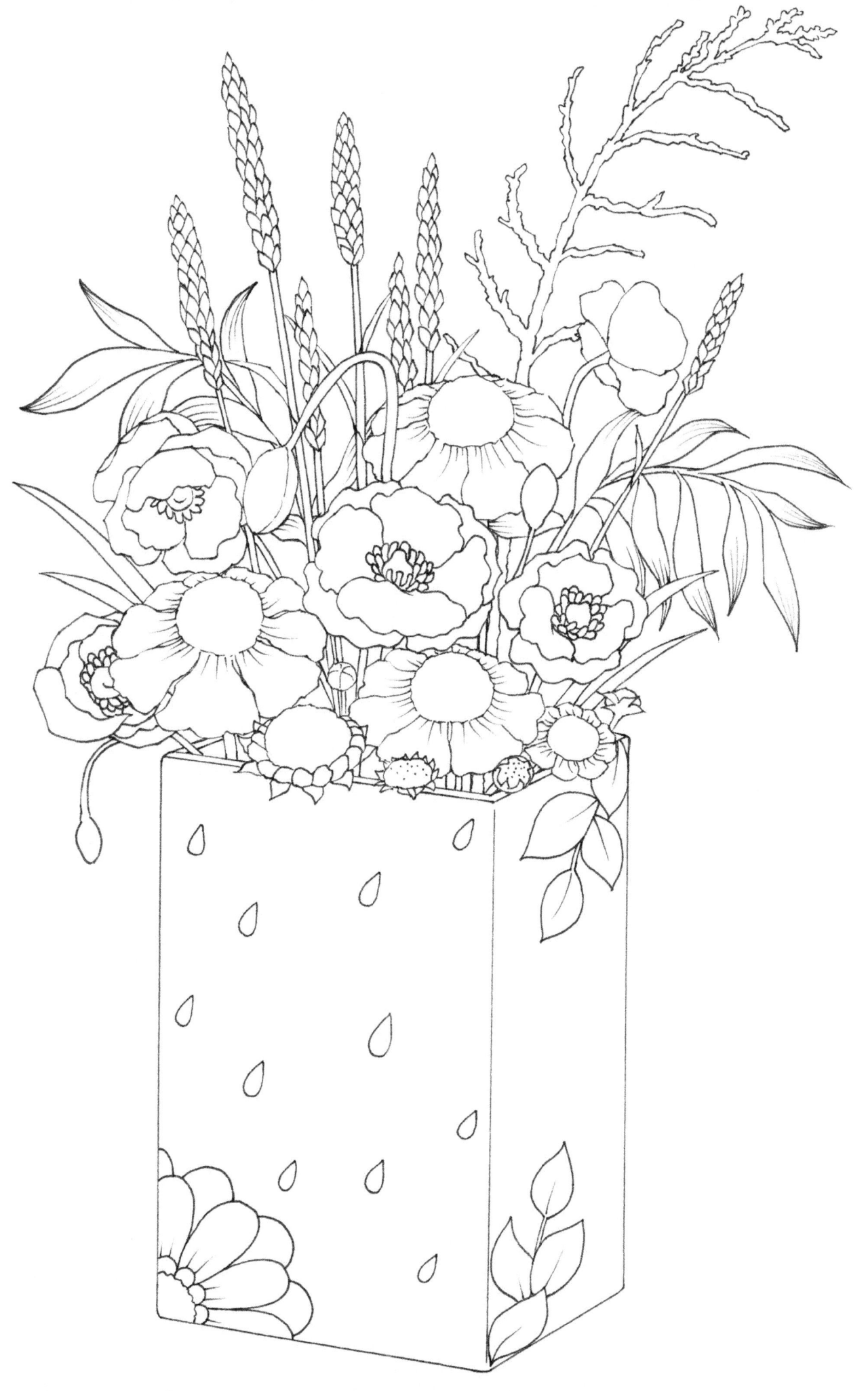

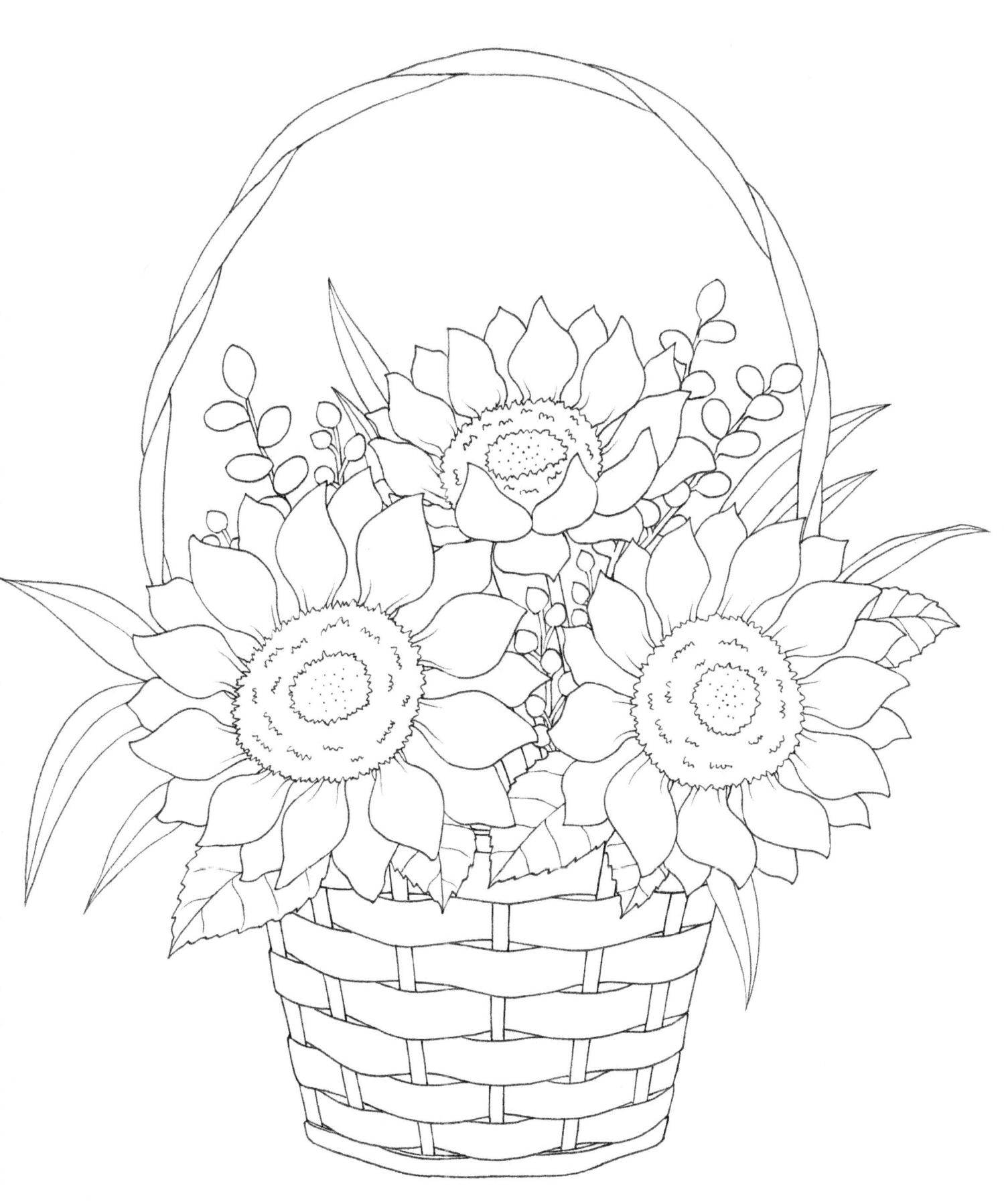

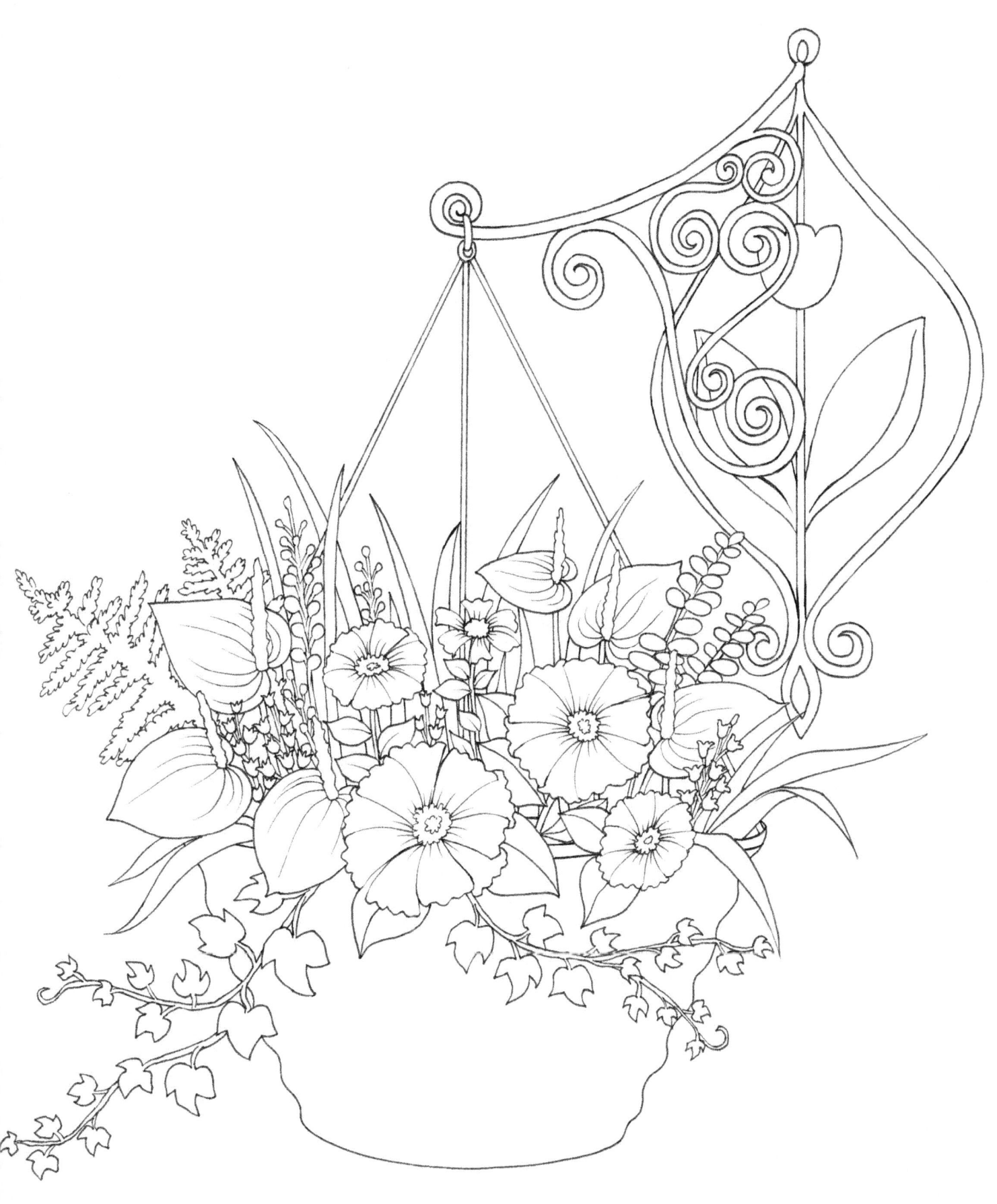

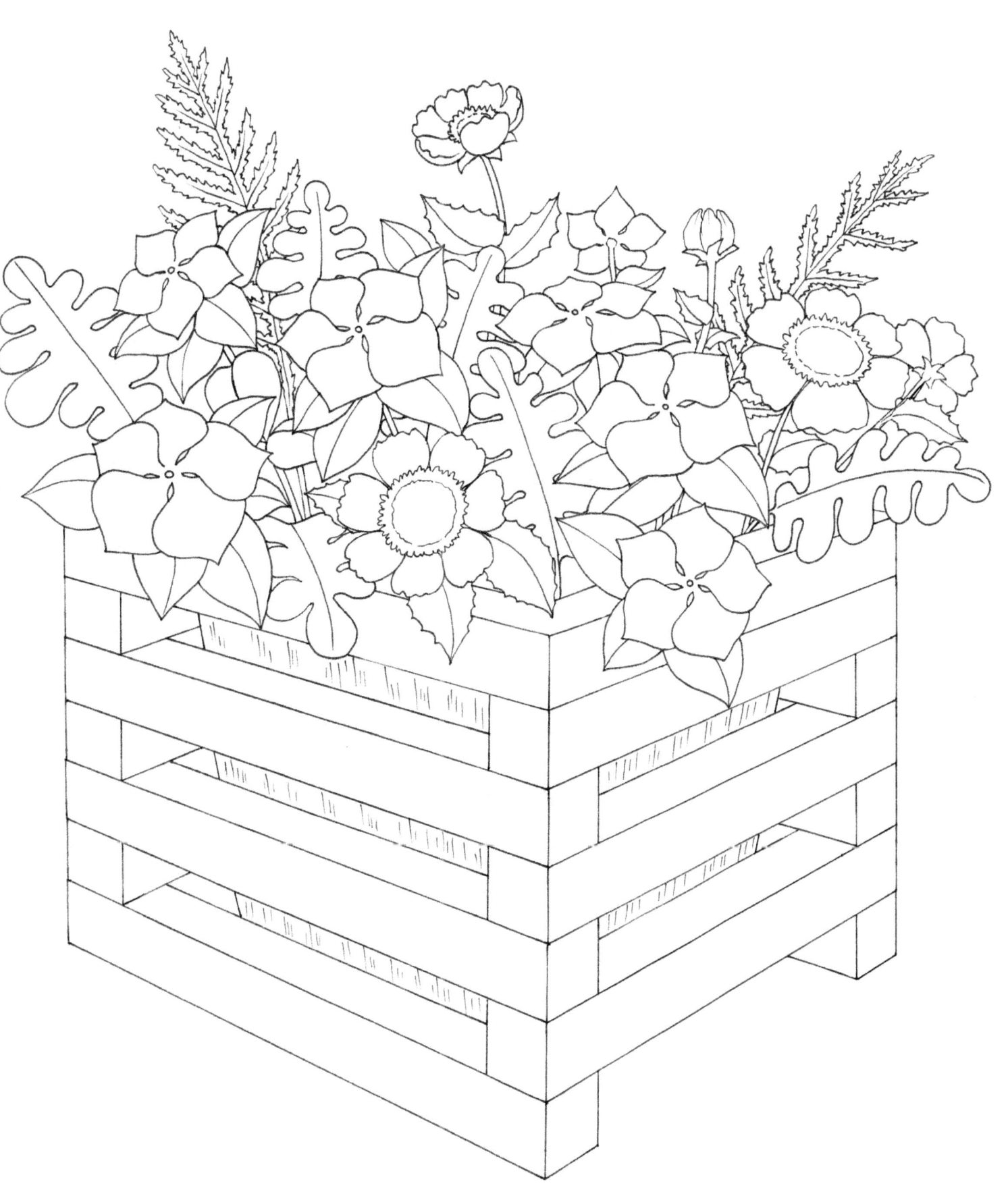

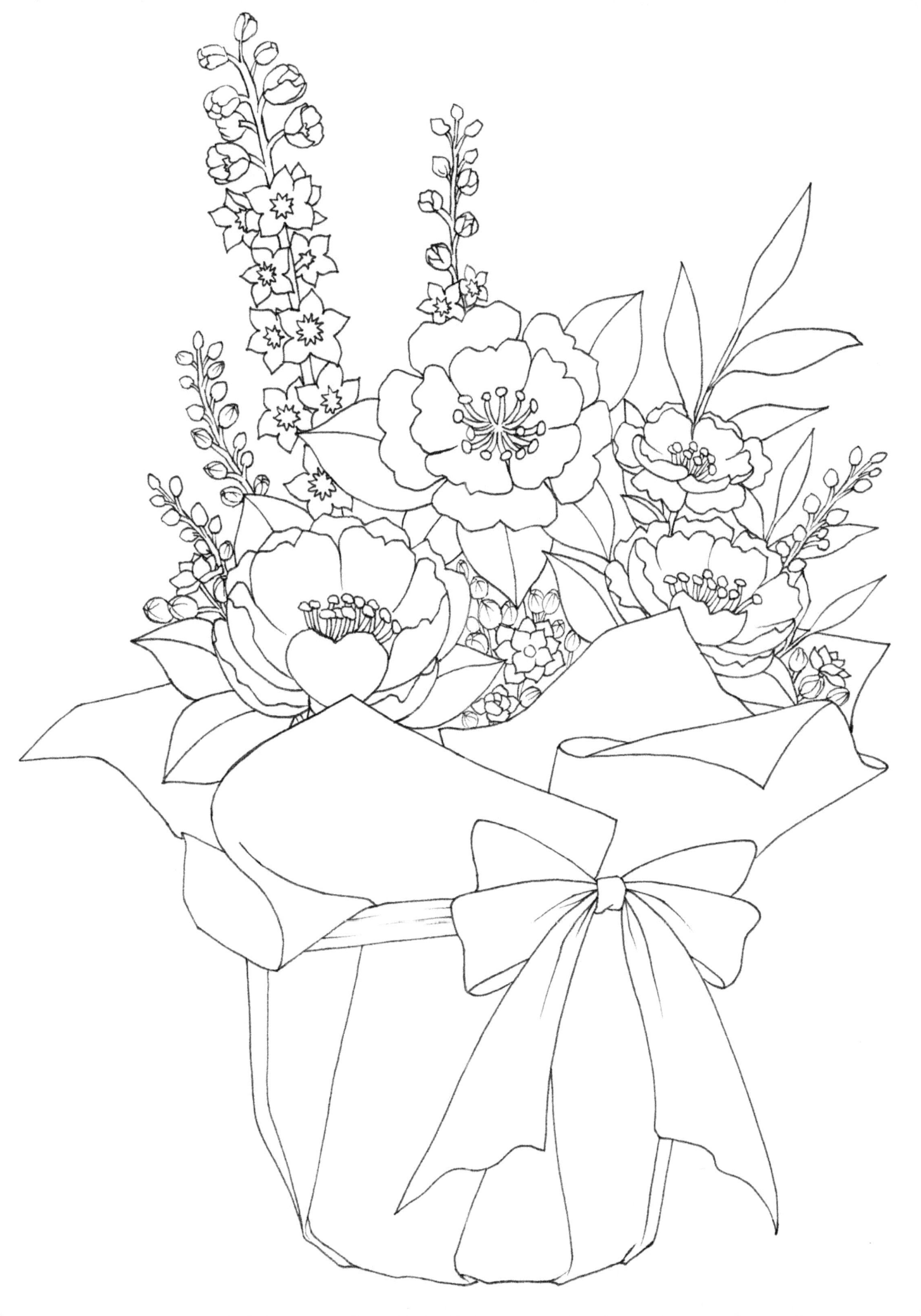

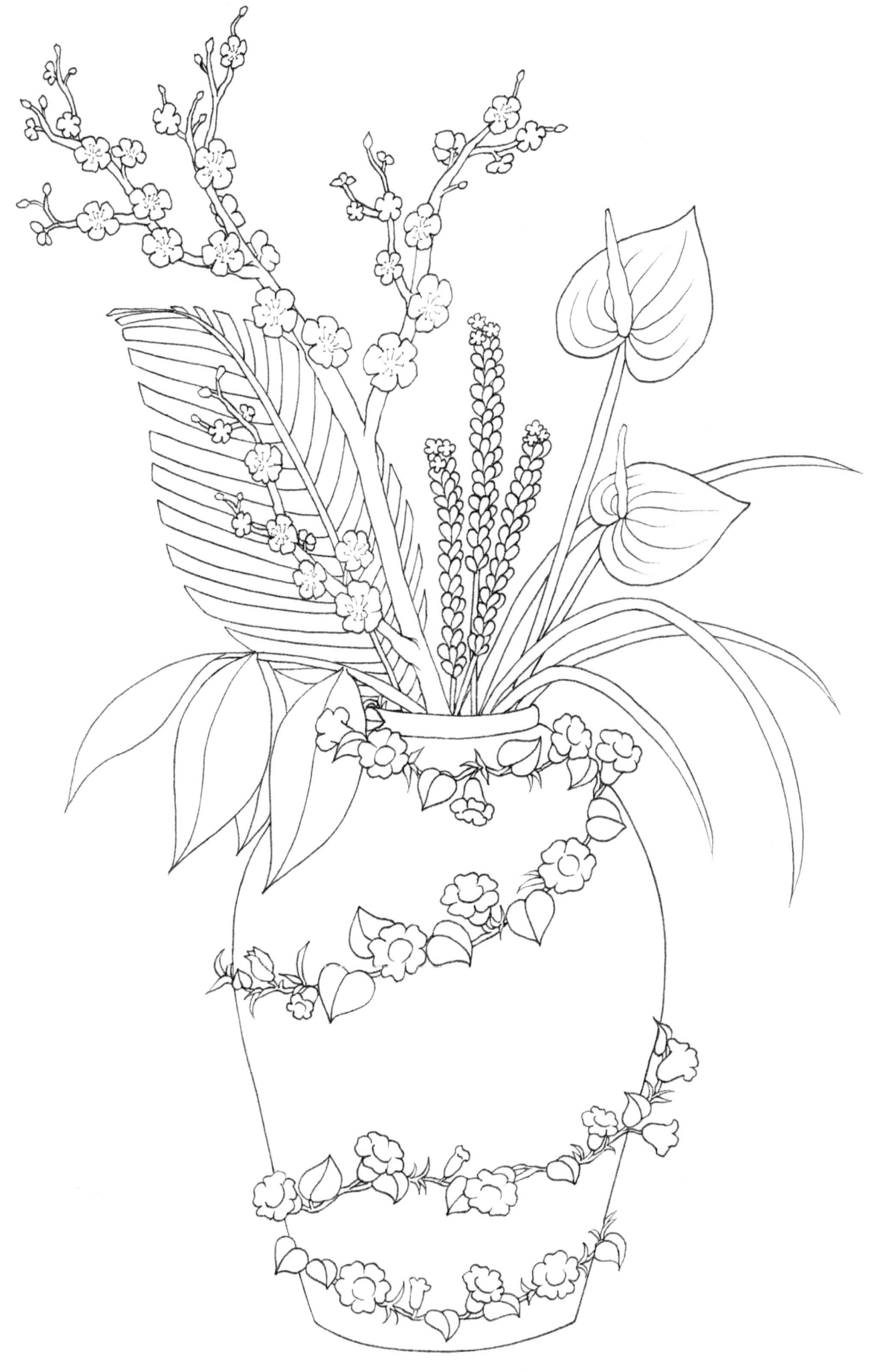

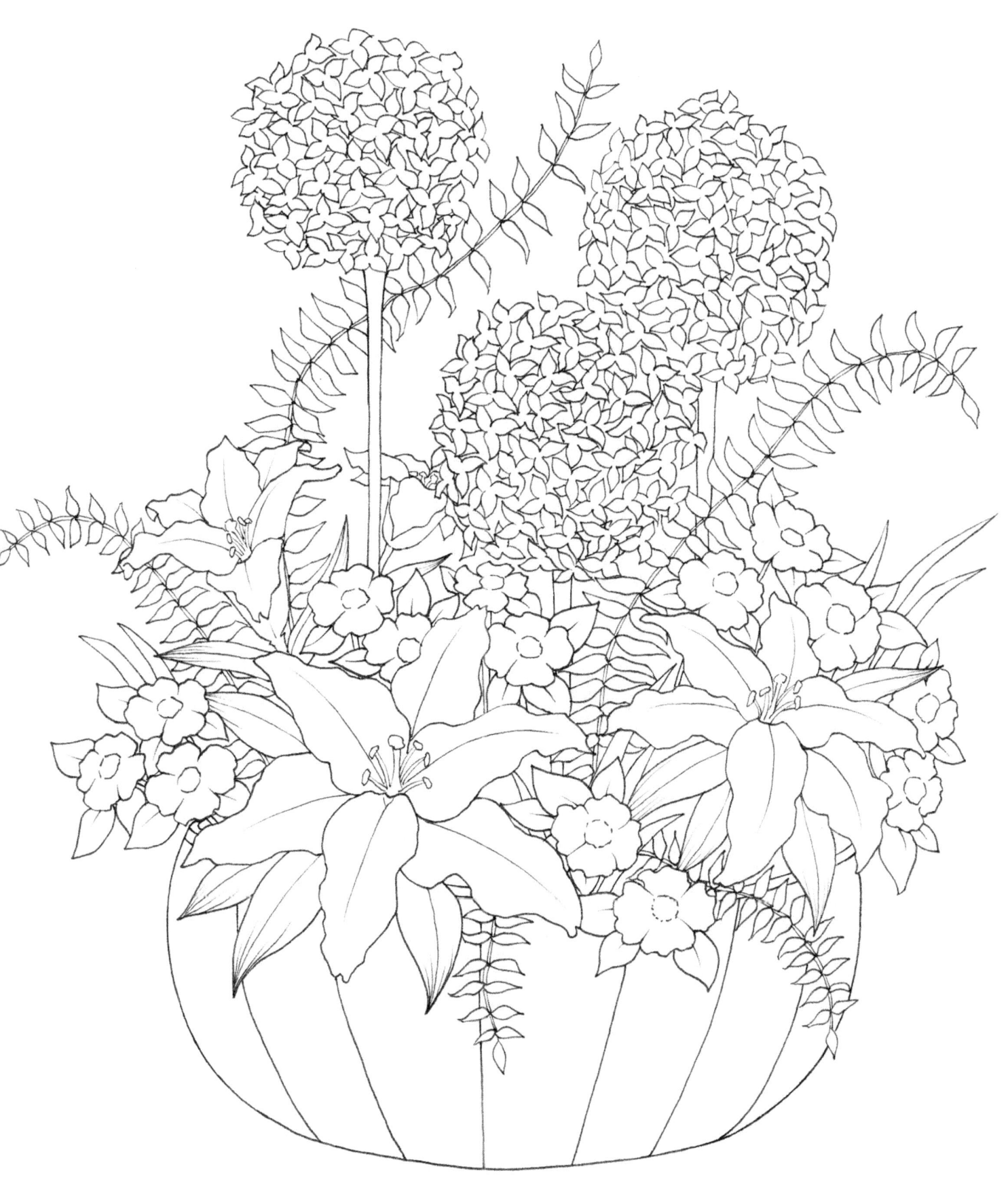

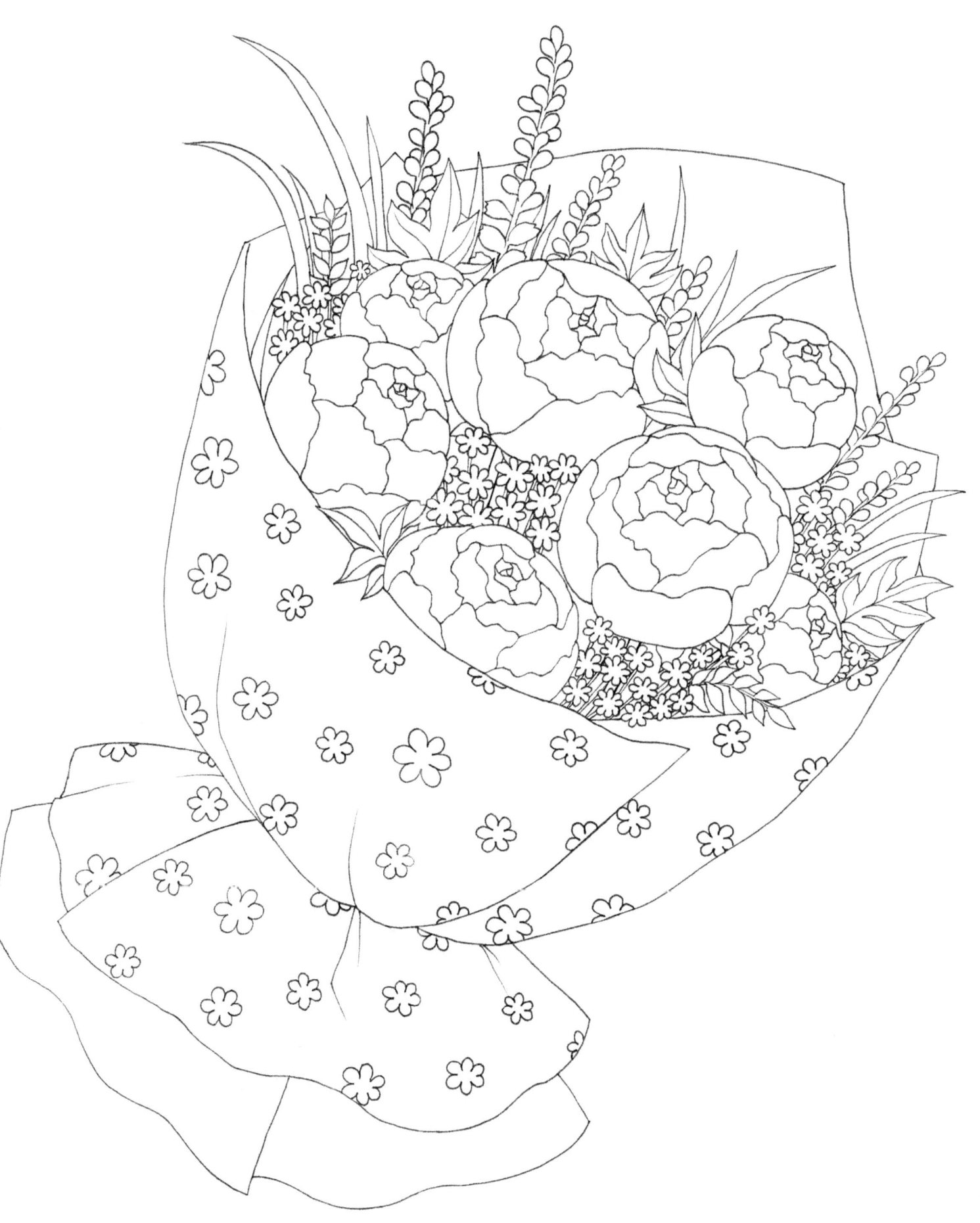

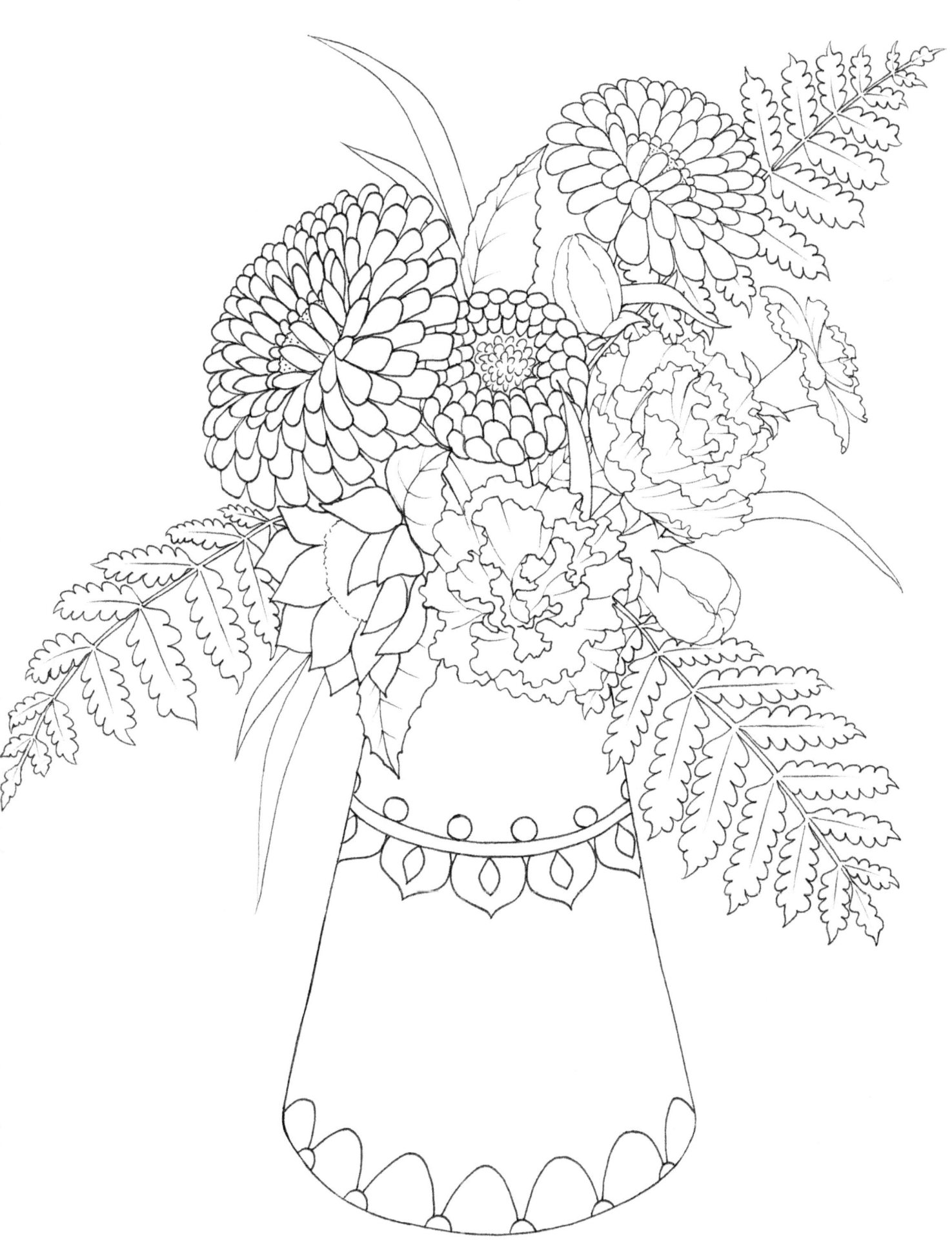

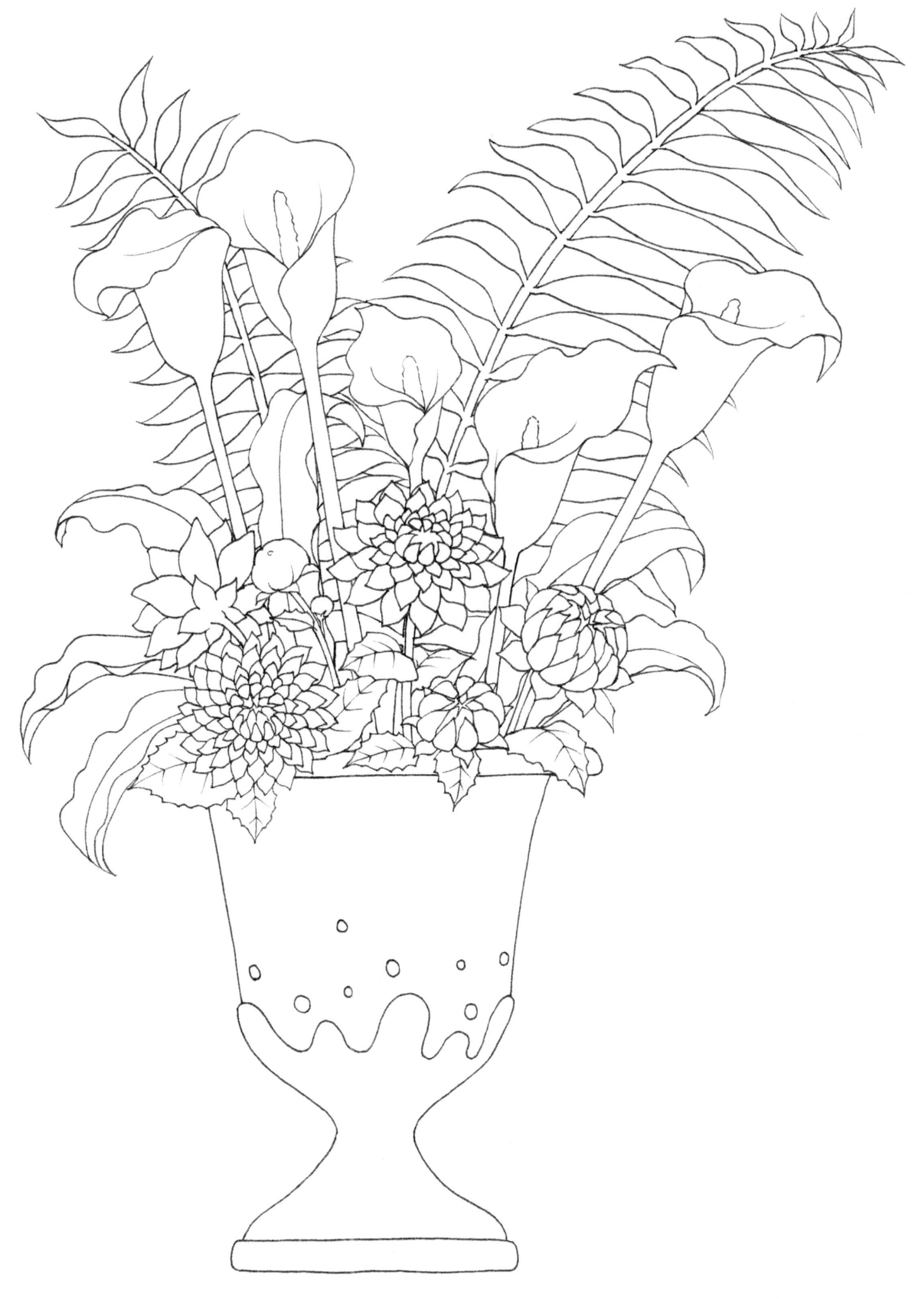

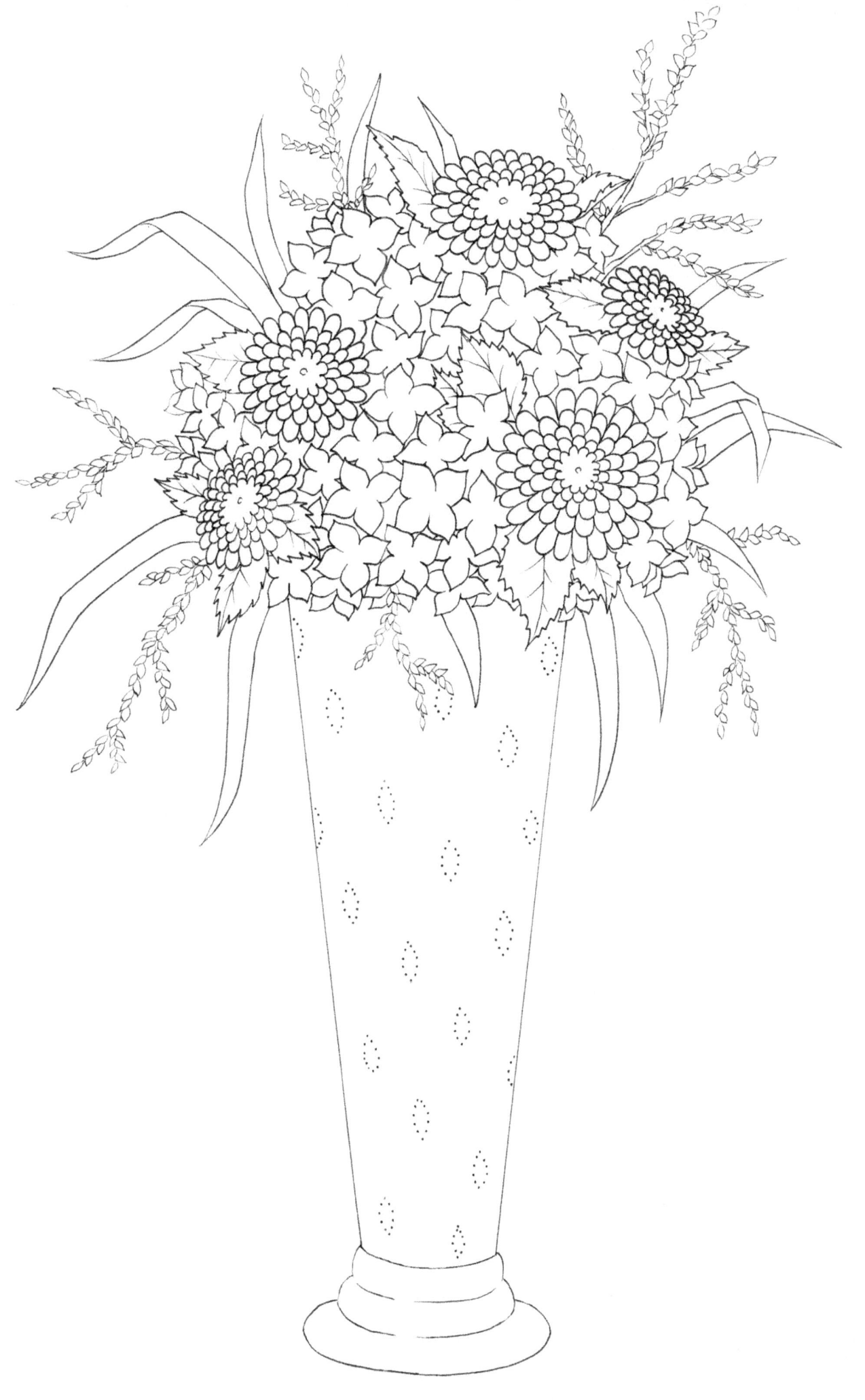